Shark in the Park

Written and illustrated by
Nick Sharratt

Down at the park,
a little boy
is testing out
his brand new toy.

Timothy Pope, Timothy Pope
is looking through his telescope.

He looks at the sky.

He looks at the ground.

He looks left and right.

He looks all around.

And this is what he sees...

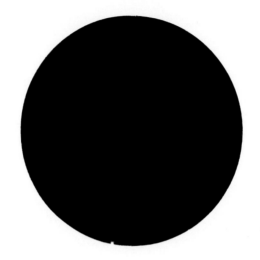

What a nasty surprise!
In his loudest voice,
young Timothy cries,

"THERE'S A SHARK IN THE PARK!"

A shark?
Fancy that!
It's only a cat.

6

**Timothy Pope, Timothy Pope
looks again through his telescope.**

He looks at
the sky.

He looks at
the ground.

He looks
left
and
right.

He looks all around.

And this is what he sees...

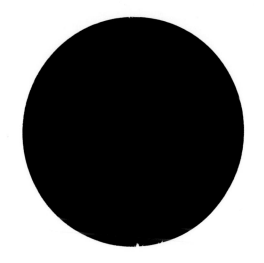

What a terrible sight!
Timothy yells
with all his might,

"THERE'S A SHARK IN THE PARK!"

A shark? Oh no!
It's just a crow.

Timothy Pope, Timothy Pope
has one more look through his telescope

He looks at
the sky.

He looks at
the ground.

He looks
left
and
right.

He looks all around.

And this is what he sees...

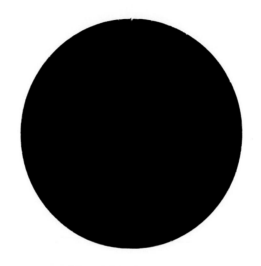

Tim's not in any doubt.
What do you think
he's about to shout?

"THERE'S A SHARK IN THE PARK!"

A shark?

That's mad!

It's Timothy's dad.

Quack!

Timothy Pope says,
"It's safe to say
there are no sharks
in the park today!"